Pat Ingoldsby occupies a unique position in Ireland. Just when you have classified him as a children's entertainer he broadcasts the kind of poems that jam RTE's switchboards.

As a playwright, his works — *H...lf...d Wh... A.. I G.. ..*
Clothes? — have been performed
Case Against The Full Shilling was
Project Theatres.

His two fantasies for children —
Yeuk were commissioned and s
Rhymin' Simon subsequently tou
Abbey Theatre banner.

RTE Radio Drama have broadca....... ... .
Australia transmitted *The Case Against The Full Shilling* in 1989.

Six collections of Pat's poems have been published to date. He regularly performs his work on radio and television. Pat has also written best selling books of zany tales for children which have also appeared on tape. His poetry readings in universities, art centres, pubs and theatres are as unpredictable as they are exciting.

He has worked on RTE Radio as a disc-jockey, made documentaries, vox-pops, hosted the *Saturday Live* T.V. chat show, written television drama for children, short stories and comedy series for radio, conceived and presented the hugely popular *Pat's Hat*, *Pat's Chat*, and *Pat's Pals* T.V. shows.

He loves rock music, soccer, Chinese food, cats and snooker. His ambition is to keep changing, to face new challenges even though they scare him, and to find peace in his head.

Scandal Sisters

PAT INGOLDSBY

ANNA LIVIA PRESS

ANNA
LIVIA

First published in 1990 by
Anna Livia Press,
21 Cross Avenue,
Dún Laoghaire,
County Dublin.

Copyright © Pat Ingoldsby, 1990
ISBN: 1 871311 08 X

Cover by Bluett
Cover photograph by Colm Henry
Typesetting: Mick Ward
Printed in Ireland by Colour Books Ltd.

Also by Pat Ingoldsby

POETRY

You've Just Finished Reading This Title
Rhyme Doesn't With Reason
Up The Leg Of Your Jacket
Welcome To My Head
Salty Water

FOR CHILDREN

Zany Tales
Tell Me A Story, Pat (cassette)

Contents

MY JOB IS GONE

When I was working
I felt good about myself
like I'd got nothing to hide,
I went out feeling nice and easy
money in my pocket gave me pride.
When I was working I never thought
that I could ever feel like this,
cut-off, alone, out of touch
trapped in a useless abyss.
I don't want to get up in the morning
I don't even want to go out
I feel that everyone is better than me
I know who they're talking about.
"Do you see him?
He's out of work
he used to be great crack,
now he avoids you
like he's ashamed
now he always watches his back."

When I was working
things were good at home
I brought in a steady weekly wage,
kept up the mortgage
new shoes for the kids
saving for retirement and old age.
Suddenly my job was gone
the company didn't want me any more,
sick in my stomach
washed-up at forty
the dole office . . . staring at the floor.
"How can we pay?
What can we do?
We need money
that we haven't got.
We'll sell the car
cancel the phone

take out a second mortgage
and then what?''

I don't feel like a man any more
I feel like a failure instead
my job gave me a sense of worth
a reason to hold up my head.
I feel like I don't belong any more
the world feels hostile and strange
I feel different to everyone else
I'm living a nightmare of change.
I hate going down to collect my dole
I feel a deep sense of shame
I'm terrified I'll meet someone I know
at hatch eleven signing my name.
When old friends meet me
and talk about work
I mutter and mumble and bluff
and make an excuse
and take to my heels
I can't get away fast enough.

I depended too much
on the job that I had
for my self-esteem and my worth
I lost sight of the fact
that I'm just as good
as anyone else on this earth.
I'm slowly realising
that cash in the bank
can never be the measure of a man.
I'm looking at myself
and the qualities I've got
and discovering the person that I am.
I'm beginning to see
that to come together
first of all I had to fall apart
and far from being finished
at losing my job
I'm actually getting a new start.

RIGHT TO BE WRONG

You *have* to be right all the time
you must never make a mistake
you must always get the right answer
a chance you must never take,
no matter what is happening
you must always be able to cope
cool and calm and in control
you must never fumble or grope.

If you ever lose your balance
and slip in a public place
leap up quickly to your feet
with composure on your face,
look around nice and easy
check that no-one has seen
now saunter along at a casual pace
laid-back and serene.

What a bloody terrible strain
always getting it right
Jesus Christ fell three times
The Titanic went down overnight
The Romans lost their Empire
John the Baptist lost his head
Adam blew it with an apple
Bo-Peep should have stayed in her bed.

What matter if you screw things up?
what harm if you make a mistake?
you've got the right to get it wrong
so give yourself a break.
Two and two is eighty six
Hong Kong is the capital of Spain
Humpty Dumpty created the world
Shakespeare wrote Penny Lane
Marconi invented the silent bang
give yourself twelve out of ten.

You're going great so far
now here we go again
half a pound of tupenny rice
is equal to twenty past three
plus the water displaced by your granny
immersed in the Caspian Sea.
It doesn't really matter
how many right answers you got
award yourself the right to be wrong
and give it your very best shot!

THE REAL YOU

It's very scary
when you go out
feeling frightened.
Everyone you see
threatens danger
everyone you see
a hostile stranger
Your legs feel like
they won't work anymore,
where to run
you can't be sure,
and fright is here
and fright is there
and no escape is everywhere
tears are welling
around your eyes
tears are massing
behind your disguise
and everybody knows
and everybody knows.

It's very scary
to sit in a cafe
feeling frightened.
Everyone you see
a dangerous stare
You feel you're
rooted to your chair.
Your voice trembles
when you try to speak
strength is gone
body weak
you want to run
you can't stand up
coffee spills
when you lift your cup
all you want to do is hide

as eyes bombard you
from every side,
and everybody knows
and everybody knows.

Force your body
tense and tight
stomach knotted
knuckles white
force it rigid
tighten the ring
voice controlled
coiled spring
Kill the trembles
mask your face
hide the tears
big disgrace
feelings buried
no-one will know
anxiety bomb
ready to blow.

Take a chance
let it be
tell your body
I've set you free
feel the fear
sense what's real
sink and enter
where you would conceal
explore your trembles
let them flow
ease your body
where it needs to go
discover what is really there
sense it
feel it
body aware
telling you
about right now

spelling out exactly how
it needs to be
listen
surrender
set it free
if people notice
what the hell
fear needs trembles
all is well
sad needs tears
anger release
emptying into
inner peace.

You'll find the people
who haven't a clue
in the face of
fearful fragile you
there's nothing in
the rules about this
so let's pretend
give it a miss.
What can we say?
What can we do?
we're not programmed
to handle you
have to dash
Love to stay
but we've lots of games to play.

You'll find the people
it's good to know
when you find the courage
to let it show
you won't even
have to explain
they've been there
they've felt your pain
they'll hold you
the natural thing to do

drawn towards the real you
easy to love
easy to care
when you are here
and they've been there.

LEAVE IT OUT

Hope that nobody comes to my door
lying stretched out on my floor,
hope that nobody rings my bell
starting to feel that all is well,
the tape is running easy and slow
relax, unwind, your tensions will go,
woman's voice softly moves
starts at my forehead
and gently grooves
through my body
on a guided tour
sinking floating
safe and sure
moving quietly
limb to limb
hushing calming
including in
all my parts
north to south
neck shoulders
tongue and mouth
my whole body
seems to float
with one exception
she seems to note
all the parts
that need to be
quiet and calm
easy and free
but relaxing tapes
don't make sense
they leave your willy
anxious and tense.

She never says it
my crucial bit
everywhere else
gets an easy hit
she names them all
personal attention
while trembling willy
is never mentioned
body calm
systems checked
willy ignored
feeling wrecked.
Rise to your feet
easy and slow
body refreshed
ready to go
tension gone
knots untangled
but down below
your willy's jangled.

I have tried to find a tape
which doesn't ignore your pistol shape
which counts him in
and calms him down
I've questioned people
all over town
relaxing tapes don't want to know
about the trembles below
it isn't there
it doesn't exist
cross if off
your body list
so at the risk
of sounding silly
I'm taking lithium
for my willy.

LEAVING CERT

Question One: "Dismantle one of your favourite poems
                 tear it apart at the seams
                 rip the words asunder
                 pause while the poet screams
                 put it under a microscope
                 dissect the little bits
                 split them with a scalpel
                 to see how each one fits
                 get a strong lump hammer
                 belt them on the floor
                 Now explain briefly why
                 you don't like it any more."

Question Two: "Now I treble dare you
                 how to blow the exam
                 answer this one honestly
                 try not to give a damn.
                 What do you really think
                 of the poems you've had to do?
                 Do you think they're any use
                 do they make any sense to you?
                 Would you bother reading them
                 if they weren't on your Leaving?
                 How many of them strike a chord
                 when you're screwed up, sad or grieving?

                 Write down exactly what you think
                 not what you've been taught to say
                 it mightn't get you honours
                 but it'll blow the crap away.

11

DON'T KEEP THIS SECRET

Sometimes grown-ups do things
that grown-ups shouldn't do
things they feel ashamed of
and they're doing them to you.
Strange things that scare you
and make you want to cry
things that pain and hurt you
and make you wish to die.

They whisper — "Keep it secret"
and give you lots of sweets
they warn you — "Don't tell Mammy
what happened under the sheets."

It's a secret that you mustn't keep
no matter how frightened you feel
good people want to help you
they care, they're near, they're real.
No matter how big the secret
no matter how scared you feel
ring your friends at Childline
they love you
they'll help you
they're real.

If you're afraid to tell your Mammy
if you're scared what Daddy will do
share your secret with Childline
they care what's happening to you.

Lots of children ring them
when they're frightened and alone
lots of children ring them
and whisper down the phone
and find a friend to listen
who knows what you can do
you've got good friends at Childline
they'd love to hear from you.

THE USUAL BALLS

Everything wrong with this country
is the other party's fault,
they did it,
we're not to blame
it's time to call a halt.
Everything right with this country
is directly thanks to us,
we did it — unselfishly,
positive with minimum fuss.
We always inherit the shambles
that the others leave behind
it's not our fault
we leave things straight
but look at what we find,
they cock things up
they tear things down
they screw us yet again
patiently we start rebuilding
with no thought for personal gain.
Our policies are constructive
responsible, courageous, true,
far-seeing, realistic
and anything else that you
can think of which sounds
impressive and strong.
Theirs are utterly mindless
negative, totally wrong.

They will lead you up the creek
down the rushy glen
deeper and deeper into debt,
deeper and deeper again,
chancing their arm
pulling the wool,
trotting out cliches and lies,
offering vague solutions
half-promises in disguise.

This is so because we say it
we say it because it is so,
WE WILL IMPROVE EVERYTHING
So baby — c'mon — let's go!
let us march together,
fearlessly
to that true native land
where everything you ever wanted
is instantly at hand,
we're not saying it's gonna be easy
but honey we ain't afraid,
'cos we . . . we got the policies,
and you . . . you got it made,
there's a bright golden haze on the meadow,
we put it there specially for you.
and God . . . God's in his heaven,
we know . . . we appointed him too.
Poppa's got a brand new bag
Momma's got a brand new gown,
social welfare's going up
inflation's comin' down.
All you really gotta do
is vote the way WE see it,
take off those shades,
pick up that pen
and groovily One . . . Two . . . Three it!

HAIL TO THEE BLITHE MONKEYS

Hail to thee blithe monkeys
I wonder if it is true,
as I gaze on your hairy bodies
am I descended from you?
Are you my distant relation
a long lost cousin or what?
How do you feel about humans
and the restricted life that you've got?
We locked you up inside a cage
how do you feel about that?
I was locked away as well
some still call me Crazy Pat,
I think you're bloody brilliant
agile and acrobatic
will we hatch an escape plan
you can hide up in my attic
I'll give you tons of bananas
mangos and curranty bread,
we'll take long walks together,
you can gawk at the people instead.

We watch you hanging upside down
and laugh at your wild high jinks
scratching and swinging around on bars
yet none of us ever thinks,
we're afraid to let ourselves go
inhibited — I'm sure you can tell
as we stand and laugh at your antics
that we're sort of caged-in as well.

I DON'T WANT TO KNOW

I think it's time
I stopped telling people
how free I feel,
because there and then,
on the spot
they give me a list
of the ways that I'm not.

"No no Pat
you've got it wrong
you might think
you're groovin' along
but you have to work
like it or not
by the chain and the balls
they've got you caught,
you have to do it
there's no escape"
there and then
they cue the tape.

"It's not like that
for me at all,"
I try and explain
I'm having a ball.

"No you're not
 you're out of touch"
It really seems
to mean so much
to make it clear
to prove to me
only security
can set me free.

"But I feel good,
I feel secure,
I live in the now
safe and sure."

"No you don't,
that's not the way
just you wait
till you're old and grey"

"But I live to write,
I write to live
I can't describe
the buzz it gives,
it's not like work
it's being whole,
a glorious fusion
body and soul,
feeling high
taking flight
nothing else
feels so right.
I'm sorry
you'll have to forgive
the life I lead
the way I live."

"You're selfish
what would we do
if everyone else
tried to live like you?
  screaming chaos
wreck the plan
  anarchy
don't give a damn"

"Oh but I do
I really do care
it's no accident
fair is fair
six breakdowns
the price I paid
and now when I feel
I've got it made
you tell me this
you tell me that
you even call me
Crazy Pat.
If this is crazy
it's bloody great
free as a bird
I just can't wait
all my tomorrows
feel no fright
happy as a hatter
and high as a kite!"

THE GLASS HOLE IN YOUR DOOR

Did anybody ever take away your clothes
and lock you in a ward where the door
only opens from the outside?
At night you hear old men saying
strange secret things to themselves.
Sometimes an eye peers through a glass hole
in the door of your room.
You don't know who's looking at you.
There's no breakfast for you on the morning
when you lie on the bed with the rubber sheet.
After the electric shock has coursed through
your head you don't have any memory for a while.
Some people think it makes you normal.
Some people think they know what normal is.

RUSSIA'S ONLY HOPE

It was the most ambitious
magnificent prayer
any of us ever said,
Brother Michael took the class
as each boy lowered his head.
We had prayed for holy purity,
one Hail Mary settled that,
we had asked for the grace
of a happy death
with a ragged Magnificat.
We had chanted the Divine Praises
that each boy would survive the test
and drift into sleep every night
with his hands crossed over his chest.
This was only the warm-up
for the major offering ahead
the class was straining at the leash
as through the Angelus we sped.
Brother Michael dramatically paused
we sensed that The Big One was near.
"LET US PRAY FOR THE CONVERSION OF RUSSIA,"
we resisted the impulse to cheer.
Anto from Sallynoggin
Marty from Fairview Strand,
all the boys from Rialto
and Mitcher from No-Man's Land,
fused into a unit
a fervent powerhouse of prayer,
passionately storming the heavens,
begging the Almighty to care.
We were determined to save them
with ten Hail Mary's a day,
we weren't too sure where Moscow was
but by God we knew how to pray.

The Protestants were in with a chance
we knew that God understood,
He'd make a generous allowance
if they did the best that they could.
We stood on the threshold of heaven
because we lived in the West
God had a map
He knew our address
we were sure of eternal rest.

We were the smallest class in the school
but we gave it our very best shot,
we knew that Inter-Cert 2C
was the only hope that they'd got.
Each morning we checked the papers
to see if we'd scored a direct hit,
25 Hail Mary's a week
plus the candles Brother Michael lit.
But the Communists were holding firm
against Inter-Cert 2C,
the Russians were laughing at our best
we hit them with the new liturgy.
Brother Michael urged us on
but little by little we knew
if they didn't want conversion
there was sweet bugger-all we could do.
The odds were stacked against us
outnumbered by thousands to one
23 boys together lost heart
and that's how the Communists won.

PICTURE

Evening so still
that I can hear
the feather flutter
of the birds
flying low
above my head
straight up goes
the winter chimney smoke.
Dropping westwards slow
slips the fiery orange ball
of fiery fading glow
and all is quiet
and all is still
and all is
wintery one.

INSIDE OUT

A little girl in the bank
purple-faced from shouting
            and screaming
                and yelling.

Her mother smacks
            holds
            shakes
        scolds her.

Gives her a pen
and a sheet of paper
sits her at a table.
Suddenly she is dry-eyed
smiling covering the page
with happy mazy scribbles.

We're still standing in the queue
                        hot
                        tired
                        fuming
        shouting and screaming
                        silently
            deep down inside.

When we reach the counter
we are all smiles
on the outside.
None of us will ever cover
a sheet of paper
with happy mazy scribbles
            ever again.

NIGHT COLD

Night cold
  ice cold
white cold
sky
stars
sharp
silver
crystal clear
sky black
sea black
sea birds
hide and pipe
     and pipe
     and hide
and lights
are green
and red
and white.

IS THAT HOW IT WAS?

And I was cool and trendy
fab and groovy and young
my hair jet black
my teeth my own
love beads all over me hung
Jagger was prancing and pouting
Bill Wyman never smiled
Lennon was twisting and shouting
The Pretty Things
outrageous and wild.
Minis and hipsters and kaftans
Beatle boots, Mary Quant styles
smoking and toking and tripping
with acid I can see for miles.

Free-love 24 hours a day
everyone getting their bit
the Kama-Sutra gone crazy
no one was going to admit
"Did I get it last night?!!
Oh yes yes yes yes yes!!!"
I spent all my time looking
I couldn't find the address.

Let's go to San Francisco
it's all happening there!
We got as far as Balbriggan,
hitched . . . we hadn't the fare.

Hare Krishna
peace brother peace
Aquarius is now
he ain't heavy he's my brother
hippies are happy and how
mods beat the shit out of rockers
rockers dismantled the mods
Sympathy for The Devil

just look what's happened our Gods,
Jesus Christ's a Superstar
J.F.K. is no more
Jimi Hendrix, Norma Jean
crumpled up on the floor.
Radio Caroline is rockin'
Montez sez let's dance
Beatles are in The Adelphi
Proby split his pants.
Psychedelic freak-out
far-out, crazy and cool
we're all gettin' high high high
Brian Jones face down in a pool.
Have you got any skins man?
Where's the party tonight?
We gotta keep on rockin'
time is getting tight.
Ottis Redding, Mama Cass,
the band is slowing down
Janis Joplin, Sam Cooke,
the show is leaving town.

The Sixties
a bloody great place to be
providing you're still around
a dizzy heady explosion
mixed with the tears of a clown.

WEATHERWORD. NUMBER ONE

"That's a great day isn't it ..."
"Did somebody tell you that?"
"Eh ... no ..."
"Well, you're the twenty-seventh who has bloody
told me ...

WEATHERWORD. NUMBER TWO

"That's a great day isn't it ..."
"Did somebody tell you that?"
"Not at all ... sure you can see it for yourself ..."
"Then why the fuck are you telling me ... ?"

THE HARDMAN RODE THE HOBBYHORSE

The hardman rode the hobbyhorse
round and round he went
mortified in Funderland,
his girlfriend relaxed and content.
"She made me get up here
Jaysus — I nearly died
It was her idea, not mine
there must be someplace I can hide."

The hardman rode the hobbyhorse
self-consciously round and round
glaring at anybody who looked
and forcing their eyes to the ground.
"I could burst you with a thump
flatten you with a belt
I hurtled on the Big Dipper
cheated death on the Helter Skelt,
the girl friend was terrified
I crashed the dodgems head-on
just smile at me on this bleedin' horse
and brother, you are gone!"

The hardman rode the hobbyhorse
staring straight ahead
no-one dared to catch his eye
they knew that they were dead
round and round on "Blossom the First"
fuming alongside the mot
"Anthrax" on the back of his jacket
and 'Clearasil' on each spot.

He rode a mustang around Cabra
bareback, fearless and wild
this bloody yoke has a plaited tail
his girlfriend secretly smiled
"He looks lovely on Blossom
If Mammy could see him now"
true love on a hobbyhorse
burstin' for a row . . .

PASSING IN THE NIGHT

I'm standing outside a pub
          on my own.
The rock gig has just finished.
A man approaches me.
"How are you Pat?"
"I'm lonely."
"Yeah but how are things?"
"I just told you — I'm lonely."
"Ah come on Pat — how's it going?"
"How often do I have to tell you?
          I'm lonely."
He looks at me and shakes his head
and walks away again.
I didn't feel quite so lonely then.

PASSING IN THE DAY

I'm walking towards the Outpatients
in St. Patrick's Hospital
feeling very screwed up.
A young guy with long blonde hair
is coming out.
"How's it going Pat?"
"I feel very screwed-up."
"Yeah — but what's the story?"
"I told you — I feel shit."
He pauses and looks at my cap.
"I've got one like that" he says.
Then he walks on.

FILL THE FAMILY ALBUM

You have to smile
whether you like it or not
smile straight at the camera
give it all that you've got
everyone else is grinning
a group of Cheshire Cats
smiling for the camera
happiness is where it's at.

Fill the family album
pack it with manic grins
page after page of happiness
the family where everyone wins.

Granny's arthritis is crippling her
she's hobbling around the zoo
mother points the camera
Granny smiles — Yoo Hoo!
Dad hasn't worked for years
his redundancy money is gone
self-esteem in his boots
say "cheese" — the flash is on.

Fill the family album
pack it with manic grins
page after page of happiness
the family where everyone wins.
They're smiling in the garden
they're smiling in the rain
they're smiling in the hospital
say "cheese" — you'll feel no pain.

Smile though your heart is breaking
do a job on your head
disguise how you're truly feeling
grin at the camera instead.
Nobody will ever know

where you're really at
how do you even start to relate
to a grinning Cheshire Cat?

Fill the family album
pack it with manic grins
page after page of happiness
the family where everyone wins
nobody ever felt miserable
unhappy confused or down
nobody ever shed a tear
sighed or wore a frown
we stood in front of the camera
smiling and anxious to please
if our lives were so bloody happy
why did we have to say "Cheese"?

WELCOME TO THE AFTERNOON

I don't want to get up today
scared in my stomach
I'd much rather stay
warm and hidden
safely in bed
afraid to get out
pressing my head
into the pillow
under the clothes
hide in the blankets
escaping from those
nagging voices
won't let me be
eyes closed
don't want to see
empty morning
emptier day
please Jesus
send it away.

Last night was safe
cushion of sleep
hoped that forever
I'd curl up and keep
the blankets around me
hide in the night
tomorrow can't get me
keep out the light
pull the curtains
draw the blinds
stick your head
up your behind
paper the cracks
barricade the door
block the chimney
you can't ignore
hands on the clock

rip them off
tomorrow is coming
I heard it cough
crept up the stairs
while you're asleep
under your door
fingers creep
for God's sake
don't open your eyes
tomorrow is here
attacked by surprise
Behind you!!!
don't turn around
daylight!!
don't make a sound
stay in the bed
pretend to snore
back to sleep
you've heard them before
nagging voices
torture your head
"You won't get a job
lying in bed
you lazy waster
negative shit
you wouldn't find
work in a fit.
When did you last
reply to an ad?
fill in a form?
the chances you've had
the money we've spent
doesn't grow on trees
if you spent a bit
more time on your knees
on your feet
out of the bed
that's right! that's right!
cover your head!!"

They've gone to work
the house is quiet
it's nearly twelve
still scared to try it
wide awake
stomach in knots
you slept for hours
and all you've got
is crumpled sheets
pillow on the floor
accusing voices
rant and roar
"Get up! Get up!
It's gone midday
you're sleeping
your bloody life away!"

Arms around your
head at war
only one thing gets
your feet on the floor
nature is calling
it won't be denied
you've knotted your legs
for hours you've tried
to shut it out
pretending to be
anything
but dying for a pee
the game is up
a man's gotta do
your cover is blown
it's twenty past two
betrayed by your body
who can you trust?
you're forced out of bed
it's piddle or bust
nowhere is safe
wee wee tinkling a tune
"Welcome to the afternoon."

YOU'RE NEVER ALONE IN YOUR PELT

There's never anybody in the hall
when you walk out of your flat
with all of your clothes on
in the house where I live.
Not a single soul do you see
all the other doors
flats one two three
four five six
are resolutely shut.
But
just you try and make a run for it
down to the showers
in your pelt
in your skin
every bloody door in the place
simultaneously opens
and faces some of whom
you have never seen before
will pack the hall
with wall-to-wall people
including a man from the ESB
who is reading the meter
and a man from Bord Telecom
who is fixing the phone
you're never alone
in your pelt
in your skin
in the hall
in the house
where I live.

GOD ALONE KNOWS

Go with the flow
try not to control it
wherever it is you need to go
the Higher Power will rock and roll it
relax into the rhythm
groove with the trip
getting there is half the buzz
enjoy it — loosen your grip
tune in to what's going on
don't leave it completely to chance
give the Almighty a bit of a hand
it takes two to dance
it's like a magical mystery tour
'till you choose where you want to go
travel there in the here and now
it's all you'll ever know
you can never leave the present
no matter how hard you try
you can only leave it in your head
and that's the reason why
flowing in the present tense
is feeling now
common sense
God alone knows where you're going to go
God . . . . . alone . . . . . knows
so relax and enjoy the flow . . . . .

SCANDAL SISTERS ARE WATCHING YOU

"She looks pregnant
she's not fooling us
baggy dresses
brazen huss
husband away
overseas
late-night callers
if you please
lights on
lights off
back door
muffled cough
heavy breathing
I heard that too
strictly between
me and you."

Gossip gossip
whisper whisper
tittle tattle
scandal sisters
sharp tongues
antennae eyes
C.I.A.
in disguise
heads together
huddled close
swapping secrets
no one knows
specialists in
local affairs
private business
is also theirs.

"He gets the bus
usual time
off to work
shoes shine
buys his paper
same routine
who's he kidding
know what I mean?
His job's gone
I happen to know
National Library
is where he goes
his poor wife
Vincent de Paul
plastic bags
I saw it all."

"Confession box
in for hours
Child of Mary
Little Flower
dark secrets
truth will out
I heard
Father Michael shout
like mother
like daughter
randy blood
thicker than water
short skirts
hours to confess
need I go on?
you know the rest."

"Haven't seen him
round for ages
down the pub
all his wages
wife and kids
tattered shoes
early pub
on the booze
she says he's gone
on a break
a holiday
he had to take
I saw the doctor
at the door
you know yourself
say no more."

Gossip gossip
whisper whisper
tittle tattle
scandal sisters
sharp tongues
antennae eyes
C.I.A.
in disguise
makes no difference
what you did
makes no difference
where you hid
makes no difference
false or true
Scandal sisters
are watching you.

THE LURKER UNDER THE BED

I expect a hand to grab me
from underneath the bed,
grab a hold of my ankle
I live in terrible dread
of being slowly dragged under
by whatever is lurking there
dragged under and gobbled up
before I can yell out a prayer.

I know there's something lurking
though it never makes a sound
it lies there and listens
with a silence that's profound.
I know there's something lurking
and making its terrible plans
to dismantle my struggling body
to rip me apart with its hands.

I spring into bed with a running jump
my body rolled up in a ball
feet tucked in under my chin
so it can't get a grip at all.
If I want to get out for a wee wee
I crouch down on the bed
and suddenly vault across the room
before it can stick out its head.

Sometimes I waken in the night
scarcely daring to breathe
my leg dangling over the edge
just asking to be grabbed from beneath.
An unguarded moment, an unguarded leg
Snatch! Grab! I'm gone!
I want a good view when it happens
so I sleep with my bedroom light on.

Doctors call it irrational
a phobia that shouldn't be there
they're welcome to spend a night in my bed
and dangle their legs if they dare.
They call my creature a figment
a product from inside my head
I promise to keep that firmly in mind
when I'm yanked in under the bed.

REVENGE IS A CREMATION CALLED BOOM

He had never made much of an impression
nobody listened when he spoke
nobody asked for his opinion
or laughed when he told a joke.
Women never noticed him
nobody remembered his face
someone else was always promoted
someone else always sat in his place.

He lay in hospital dying
nobody sat by his bed
for once he felt relieved
for a plan whizzed around in his head.
He hollowed out a suppository
and packed it with gunpowder tight
then he cheerfully stuck it up his arse
and absorbed it out of sight.

"T'will be a cremation to remember"
he whispered as life faded fast
then he grinned a manic sort of grin
and happily breathed his last.

EAR TO EAR

I feel very sad because
my ears have never met,
a bloody big head between them
is as close as they're going to get.
My toes all groove together
my teeth live side by side,
but my ears are total strangers
'cos my head's so bloody wide.
They live in isolation
under my straggely hair
in fact I sometimes wonder
do they know that the other one's there.

I SAW TWO MEN HOLDING HANDS

I saw two men holding hands today
and I averted my eye
and I looked the other way
so that they wouldn't see me
seeing them.
I walked on quickly and
I felt strangely strange.

Two men deeply in love
holding hands as lovers do
feeling good and warm
and very very happy.
I was the one who felt freaked
and something else too
very very envious of two people
who've got the courage
to say to the world
"Look . . . this is my lover
this is my special person
who I choose for me
and I don't need your permission
and I don't need your approval
and I don't need your consent
and I don't need your poems.
All that I need is my lover's love
and that is more than enough for me.
I don't ever tell you what you should
and shouldn't do.
I don't ever tell you who you should
and shouldn't love.
I'm easy and I'm happy holding hands
. . . . how are you?''

PARTNER DECIDED ON RIVER PIKE

Partner decided on river pike
with a saffron scented sauce
we sipped our Perrier Jouet N.V.
we really felt at a loss,
couldn't decide between champagne
or Ballygowan water,
not easy . . . a sudden impulse
become a Ballygowan martyr.

Cornflakes for the breakfast
Oh Jesus — the bread is hard
Jason — scrape the margarine
else we're down to the lard
Daddy had the sausage
He gave Natalie a bit
an apple for lunch at school
my stomach's an empty pit.

The white chocolate truffle
left a lot to be desired
eh — wasn't quite chocolatey enough
the chef was less than inspired.
Full marks to the brandy coffee
it subtly excited the tongue
the conversation was sparkling
Spring lamb was perky and young.

No money for the bus fare
E.S.B. is gone again
have to walk it into town
pray it doesn't rain
Natalie needs a pair of shoes
I need a bleedin' job
Jesus Christ I'd love a pint
Brother — can you spare a bob?

The bill was eighty pounds fifty
quite reasonable for two
Service was twelve and a half per cent
the colour scheme was blue
we both agreed on the brussel sprouts
inclined to be a bit too firm
didn't exactly spoil the meal
although partner was seen to squirm.

Amanda — you take the bag of crisps
and don't eat them on the way
Mark — go easy on the milk
it has to last all day
Jason — stop biting your nails
and finish your slice of toast
bread doesn't grow on trees
God — I'd devour a Sunday roast.

Blessed are the poor
they shall inherit the earth
blessed is the bag of crisps
and food from the breast at birth
Blessed is the ambience
enhanced with coffee cream
blessed is the bedroom
where empty tummies dream.

WHO WAS THAT MAN IN A THREE-PIECE SUIT?

I will never feel scornful
towards a man in a suit again
because you never know who
you are scorning.

Last week at lunchtime in St. Stephen's Green
while all the office workers were enjoying
their temporary release
suddenly without warning
a baby bird fell out of its nest
and plummeted to the ground.

A man in a three-piece suit ripped it off
with a dramatic ripping sound
and holy shit — he was well and truly
                Superman!!!
He soared up and caught the little bird
and kept right on soaring
while tongues of fire descended
on the ducks in the ornamental pond
and Countess Markievicz statue said
"This is my beloved son in whom I am well pleased."
And Superman — the fourth person of The Blessed Trinity
was assumed into heaven.

I will never feel scornful
towards a man in a three-piece suit again
because you never know who you are scorning.

LEAVE THE TAPE RUNNING

"Nonsense" they said.
"It's so much safer
than travelling by car.
Look how often you travel by car
and it doesn't cost you a thought."

"I never looked at it that way before" he said.

"Statistics prove it" they said.
"Thousands of planes
flying millions of miles
without even a burst tyre."

"By God — you're perfectly right!" he said.
"Get me a taxi to the nearest airport."

When they finally found The Black Box
none of this conversation was recorded on it.

HOW IT REALLY IS

I'm alive and I've got rights
I've got the right to live my life
the way that I want it to be.
I've got the freedom to say
"This is my dream and I've got
all the resources and all the strength
that I need to make it happen."

I don't have to settle for
anything or anybody that I don't want.
I don't have to stand helplessly by
and watch other people
making their dreams happen.
I am not trapped in anything I don't want.

If anybody says to me
"No — don't do that
you won't be able to do it."
I have the freedom and the right
to say "Fuck off and take your
negative shit with you!"
If anybody says to me
"No No — that mightn't work
don't try that."
I have the freedom and the right
to say "Blow it out your arse!"

If anybody's weight is too heavy for me
I have got the right to say
"Your weight is too heavy
get off my fucking back."
If my weight is too heavy for me
I have the right to say to me
"Hey hey Pat — easy
take it easy
there are enough deadbeats out there
who will happily screw you up
without you doing a demolition job
on yourself.
If you declare war on yourself
you may as well quit before
you even start."

I have got the right
to give myself full permission
to make my life
easy and good for me
I have got total freedom to say
"This is how I want my life to be"
and I have got all the resources
that I need
to make it happen
so hello freedom
        hello dreams
        hello life
I very nearly lost you.

THE WRINGLETHUMPS ARE IN

They never miss a first-night
they go to all the shows
Lord and Lady Wringlethump
in their expensive clothes
prowling around the foyer
eyes alert and alight
Lord and Lady Wringlethump
searching for someone to bite.

They carefully select a victim
and stalk him through the throng
humming gently under their breath
humming the biter's song
"Hi diddle dee dee
A biter's life for me
bite the shin
bite the bum
a biter's work is never done."

They crouch behind their victim
waiting till the time is right
then they release a blood-curdling howl
and give him an unmerciful bite.
Lord and Lady Wringlethump
at every glittering affair
nobody stands near them
people take enormous care
never to expose their bottoms
or leave an unguarded shin
word flashes round like wildfire
"The Wringlethumps are in!"

Lord and Lady Wringlethump
keep a count of their sins
a very precise tally
of bitten bums and shins
they favour foyers with potted plants
and things to crouch behind
they crawl around under the seats
never knowing where they'll find
a bulging bum, a tender shin
Beware Beware — The Wringlethumps are in!

If you ever go to a first-night
stand with your back to the wall
borrow a pair of shin-pads
and strain your ears for the call
that petrifies first-nighters
sets hearts thumping within
it's a loud call and a clear call
"The Wringlethumps are in!"

HEY YOU WITH THE PONY TAIL

Spare me from drunks
who are having a ball
and think you should be doing the same
"Hey you . . . come on . . . get up and dance
Hey you . . . eh . . . whatshis name,
what are you sittin' there for?
get up and let yourself go,
come on Jimmy . . . shake a leg
are ye gettin' up . . . yes or no?"

Spare me from drunks
who are feeling happy
and think that you should be too
"Hey Jimmy — you'll be a long time dead
hey misery guts . . . yeah — you,
cheer up . . . it might never happen"
he's spilling the pint in his hand
"Hey you . . . come on — be happy"
the guy can hardly stand.

Spare me from drunks
who are feeling no fear
and are ready to fight to the death
"Hey you — what are ye lookin' at?"
bleary-eyed brewery breath.
"Hey you with the pony-tail
you think you're bleedin' great
hey you — does your mother stitch?"
the guy can hardly stand straight.

Spare me from drunks
who are hitting it hard
and think you should get plastered too,
"Hey you — you with the orange
d'ye know what I want you to do?
would you ever have a proper drink
orange won't do you no good,
get a proper drink down you
and get plastered like real men should."

I don't tell people when to dance
I don't tell them what to drink
I never tell people to cheer themselves up
I don't tell them what to think.
If that's what boozing does for you.
if that's what it makes you do
I'm sticking with the orange
and I'm keeping well clear of you.

MARTY SCORCHES THE SEATS

"Don't, Marty, Don't" said the girl at the pictures,
She really meant "Do, Marty, Do,"
He was at the exploratory stage
his right hand down near her shoe,
spying out the lie of the land
inspecting for buttons and zips,
finishing off preliminary checks
eagerly licking his lips.

It's a gradual progression
no need to hurry or push it
the night is young and so is he
throttle back — no need to rush it.
Manouevering into position
seeing how far he could go
how many things he could open
before she said "No Marty No!"

If you were sitting behind them
so far you'd never guess
it's all very secret and subtle
a finely measured undress.
Now they move closer together
their silhouettes merge into one
as in the cinema's shadows
things are unzipped and undone.

Marty begins to invade her space
Operation Over The Top,
he knows she means "Go Marty Go!"
when she whispers "Stop Marty Stop!"
One seat isn't large enough
for what he's got in mind
you don't know where to be looking
if you're sitting directly behind.
You can't tell who owns what,
or which bit belongs to who
you try to keep your eyes on the screen
it's a bloody hard thing to do
when a couple is gasping and panting
they sound like an asthma attack
the Kama Sutra is really confusing
when you're viewing it from the back.

Marty's bottom rises up in the air
impossible to ignore,
Although like a good snooker player
he keeps one foot on the floor.
He's searching for the Holy Grail
I think he wants to test it,
if the cinema lights come on now
this pair'll be arrested.
The film is classified P.G.
where nothing naughty is seen
if you want to sit behind Marty
you better be over eighteen.
The cinema cleaners find coke tins
pop-corn and wrappers from sweets
Marty finds The Stairway to Heaven
and leaves scorchmarks on the seats.

CHILD IN BLACK

Short black skirt
bold black tights
rich red lips
late late nights
eighteen years
model pose
sultry mask
no-one knows
Daddy's girl
very lost
running scared
fingers crossed
laughing loud
drinking hard
happy front
emotions scarred.

Dressed to kill
designer gear
designer drinks
drown the fear
flashing lights
jungle beat
find the place
where trendies meet
cover girls
glossy guys
front page looks
money buys

shaping posing
looking good
having a ball
like groovies should
eighteen years
live or bust
another guy

bites the dust
set them up
shoot them down
glossy guy
hits the ground
dressed to kill
highest bid
pays for what
her Daddy did
lead them on
lips of red
set them up
shoot them dead.

Eighteen years
living wild
shiny front
frightened child
needing love
getting lost
running scared
fingers crossed
in-crowd
place to hide
laugh a lot
cry inside
need love
need it bad
need love
never had
in-crowd
place to be
someone please
rescue me.

BLOW IT OUT YOUR BAROMETER

"No man is an island"
That's what his therapist said.
"What you need to do is meet
and mix with other people.
Interact, communicate, chat,
listen and grow,
That's your project for today
so off you go."

"But . . . I don't know
how to start, what to say,
to make anybody want to stay."

"That's your project,
off you go, chat, listen,
communicate and grow."

"Eh . . . hello . . . . . ."

"Howya — that's not a bad day now,
a bit better than yesterday although
it didn't start off too well, mind you
we can't complain, as long as we don't
get the rain we're not doing too badly
now are we?"

"Eh . . . hello . . ."

"There ye are . . . it's picking up
nicely now isn't it, a bit chilly
earlier on but sure I suppose you
can't have everything, once it's dry
that's the main thing and it's quite
nice really once you get out of the wind."

61

27 hellos later he was the best informed person
on the subject of the weather in the entire country.
One informant told him it had been the
hottest day for eighty years in Athens.
One informant told him it was thanks to the Ozone Layer.
Three people gave him graphic word pictures of the
        winter of 1947.

27 Weather bulletins later he went back to his therapist
and told him to blow it out of his barometer.
Then he returned to his island.
It was pissing rain there but
he felt deliriously happy
because there was nobody else
on the island to tell him that.

LOVELY TO MEET YOU

I met you on the train today
and almost immediately
you talked about your
membership of A.A.
I loved your openness
and your honesty.
I told you about
my fear of change and
you gave me a mint.
You talked about your
husband's death last year
and I gave you a photograph
for your grandchildren.

We only met for five minutes
and for five very beautiful minutes
I really met you
and you really met me
and it was bloody lovely.
That is why I kissed you
when we reached my station.

I've just realised it now,
six or seven hours later,
we didn't mention the weather once.

We didn't need to.

WILLOW — THE PUSSIES' DELIGHT

He turns up his collar
pulls down his brim
no other pussy cat
is as natty as him.
He brushes his jump suit
ginger and furry
his after-shave tingles
he's groovy and purry.
Pussy Willow
is going out tonight
all the lady pussies
are gonna feel alright.
He sits on the wall
and sniffs the night air
laid-back and lazy
Willow hasn't a care
all the lady pussies
are gonna stand in line
'cos no one's like Willow
Willow does it just fine.
He never leaves his number
no forwarding address
he twitches his whiskers
and all the pussies answer yes.
Willow's got charisma
Willow's got the glow
the pistol-packin' tomcat
every pussy wants to know.
In and out of the shadows
flitting along the wall
from Siamese to alley cats
Willow's had them all
home in time for breakfast
a wash, a stretch, a yawn,
curling up, closing eyes
going . . . going . . . gone . . .

THE MIRACULOUS CASE OF NATHAN'S EXPANDING NOSE AND HIS ALLERGIC WILLY

Whenever Nathan feels turned on
nothing happens down below
his willy remains asleep
but his nose begins to grow.

It simply gets longer and longer
before his very eyes
Nathan thinks about ice-cubes
to bring it back to size.

His willy has a crisis of confidence
and a personality freeze
it's allergic to cats and feathers
and pollen makes it sneeze.

Nathan deeply disturbs the public
and causes traumatic scenes
when "it" unleashes a loud atishoo
from deep inside his jeans.

Nathan doesn't know where to look
it really can depress you
when your willy does a powerful sneeze
and a woman says "God bless you."

He can't bring his nose to the pictures
or he'll sit in mortal dread
it'll suddenly lose the run of itself
and tip the back of somebody's head.

The specialist was wide-eyed
he phoned his friends when Nathan was gone
"I swear it! A sneezing willy!
and a nose that gets turned on!"

Nathan has devised a stratagem
for when summer pollen blows
a smog-mask in his trousers
and an ice-pack on his nose . . . . .

A NATHAN'S GOTTA DO

Nathan went downtown today
looking for something to do
he stood beside the roadworks hole
and all at once he knew.
He felt a sense of purpose
as he read the roadworks sign
"We apologise for the inconvenience"
his life was transformed by that line.

He walked up to the burliest man
who rattled a pneumatic drill
he tapped him on the shoulder
and shouted clear and shrill
"Don't worry! I forgive you!"
and he pointed to the sign
"For your penance say three Hail Marys
and your drilling will turn out fine."

Nathan filled up with mercy
and so it came to pass
he went on to forgive the ESB
Bord Telecom and Dublin Gas.
He wandered around the roadworks
and he read their apology sign
then he gave them each a penance
or else he imposed a fine.
Some of them told Nathan
exactly what he could do
but Nathan smiled gently
and Nathan forgave them too.

Tomorrow he's off to the Airport
where they "Apologise for the delay"
he can't wait to forgive a Jumbo jet
with an "Ego absolvo te",
a quick call to Heuston Station
to forgive a train or two
then on to Busaras
before his day is through.

This man doesn't spare himself
he's honest, steadfast and true,
because a Nathan's got to do
what a Nathan's gotta do . . . . .

WHEN THE GROPING HAS TO STOP

If someone starts to fool with you
they can't keep their hands to themself
and when you don't play along
they jeer — "You'll be left on the shelf,"
If you dread going into work
because of the things they do
you don't have to take it
your body belongs to you.

They hide behind suggestive remarks
sly touches, grabs and gropes
a word, a look, a hint, a feel,
each workplace molester hopes
you'll be too scared to confront them
nobody likes to be jeered
they'll call you old-fashioned and frigid
a kill-joy, a spoilsport, weird.

Take a deep breath and report it
you've got the right to say 'Stop',
it's not easy when you're feeling freaked
in the office, the factory, the shop.
They'll argue — "Can you not take a joke?"
as if something's the matter with you
they'll try to put you in the wrong
in spite of the things that they do.
You don't have to take it,
the law is on your side,
you've got the right to demand respect
when respect is being denied.

If the boss is abusing his position
using you for his sexual play
hiding behind his office door
brightening up his day.
You don't have to take it
you're not on your own
it's happening all over
and nothing can condone
sexual bullies and cowards
who feed upon your fear
you're not asking for a favour
your right is simple and clear
respect in your workplace
respect wherever you go,
make a start with one strong word
make a start with NO.